Coastal Inspirations

"Most of us look at a thing and believe we have seen it, yet what we see is only what our prejudices tell us to see, or what our past experiences tell us should be seen, or what our desire wants to see. Very rarely are we able to free our minds of thoughts and emotions, and just see for the simple pleasure of seeing. And so long as we fail to do this, so long will the essence of things be hidden from us."

BILL BRANT, BRITISH PHOTOGRAPHER

Volume Copyright ©2013 Marissa O'Neil & Peter O'Neil
Photographs ©2013 Peter O'Neil

Published by Vineyard Stories
52 Bold Meadow Road
Edgartown, MA 02539
508 221 2338
www.vineyardstories.com

Greg Anderson quoted from *The 22 Non-Negotiable Laws of Wellness*, 1995, printed with permission, HarperCollins Publishers, NY.

Melody Beattie quote printed with permission of the author.

Joseph Campbell quote "By permission of Apostrophe S Productions, from *Joseph Campbell and the Power of Myth with Bill Moyers*—available on DVD."

Arthur C. Clark quote from *Hazards of Prophecy: The Failure of Imagination*, in the collection *Profiles of the
Future*, 1965, revised 1973, printed with permission HarperCollins Publishers, NY.

Louise Hay quote printed with permission of the author.

Sam Keen quote printed with permission of the author.

Helen Keller quote *Courtesy of the American Foundation for the Blind, Helen Keller Archives.*

David McCullough quote printed with permission, Simon & Schuster Inc., NY.

Doug Pagels quote printed with permission of Blue Mountain Arts, Boulder, CO.

Derek Walcott poem *Love After Love*, printed with permission, from *Collected Poems 1048-1084*, 1986, by Farrar, Straus, & Giroux, NY.

David Whyte poems printed with permission from Many Rivers Press, Langley, Washington. www.davidwhyte.com

Every effort has been made to trace the ownership of all copyrighted material, and to secure permission from the holders of the copyright. If we have
failed to acknowledge any copyright holder, we apologize for the inadvertent error, and will be happy to make the correction in subsequent printings.

Library of Congress Control Number: 2013931808
ISBN: 978-0-9849136-5-7

Book Design: Jill Dible, Atlanta, GA

Printed in China

Coastal Inspirations

DRAWING BEAUTY AND MEANING FROM THE SEA

Marissa O'Neil & Peter O'Neil

VINEYARD STORIES
Edgartown, Massachusetts

Introduction

This book is a collaboration of a father and daughter, thirty-three years apart, who make a yearly voyage to the Martha's Vineyard sea shore—a time that has been a foundational family event. These trips have made the coast a place where time stops and our worries lighten. This sanctuary has provided our family a place where, despite how life's choices have empowered us to grow independently, we come together to connect on a deeper level and create shared memories.

This is where we call home.

This is where we have felt inspired—our lives magnified and deepened until we have felt clarity of vision, emotion, and purpose.

Coastal Inspirations is our opportunity to give you the same gifts the sea has given us.

We have paired photographs and quotes designed to capture a single moment along life's journey while presenting a sense of timelessness and universality. They are meant to prod memories, aspirations, and directions in life. The images are ones that elicit pause and reflection, conveying insight, initiating a conversation and inspiring action. Some of the pairings are clear and unambiguous. Others are elusive. All are intended to resonate with you on life's pilgrimage.

Our own journey in creating this book has helped transform our parent-child role into one of colleagues, sharing the work and challenging each other on a daily basis. We are using our new relationship and what we have learned from this book to align ourselves with living at the edge.

We believe this collection of images and words creates a tapestry that will enrich your passage to discover what brings you alive.

Turn these pages and open your heart to the journey within yourself.

Bon voyage,
Marissa and Peter

"The only **journey**
is the journey **within**."

RAINER MARIA RILKE

"How can we **know who we are** and where we are going if we don't know anything about **where we have come from** and what we have been through?"

DAVID McCULLOUGH

"There are, it seems, two muses:
the **Muse of Inspiration**, who gives us
inarticulate visions and desires, and the
Muse of Realization, who returns again and
again to say, 'It is yet more difficult than you
thought.' It may be that when we no longer
know what to do, **we have come to our real
work** and when we no longer know which
way to go, **we have begun our real journey.**"

WENDELL BERRY

"Whatever you can do or **dream you can**, begin it. Boldness has **genius, power and magic** in it!"

JOHANN WOLFGANG VON GOETHE

"People say that what we're all seeking is a **meaning for life**. I don't think that's what we're really seeking. I think that what we're seeking is an **experience** of being alive, so that our life experiences on the purely physical plane will have **resonances** with our own innermost being and reality, so that we actually feel the **rapture of being alive**."

JOSEPH CAMPBELL

"You would be wise to listen to the **wisdom of a tree:** Live your life with your own personal majesty. Let the **roots of all your dreams grow deep**. Let the hopes of all your tomorrows grow high. **Bend, but don't break**. Take the seasons as they come. Stick up for yourself. And **reach for the sky**."

DOUG PAGELS

"Far away in the sunshine are my **highest aspirations**. I may not reach them, but I can look up and **see their beauty, believe** in them, and try to follow where they **lead**."

LOUISA MAY ALCOTT

"Don't ask yourself what the world needs. Ask yourself **what makes you come alive** and then go do that. Because what the world needs is people who have come alive."

HOWARD THURMAN

"The future belongs to those who **believe in the beauty of their dreams.**"

ELEANOR ROOSEVELT

"If you have built **castles in the air,** your work need not be lost; that is where they should be. Now **put the foundations under them.**"

HENRY DAVID THOREAU

"Go confidently in the direction of your dreams. Live the life you've imagined."

HENRY DAVID THOREAU

"A man **travels the world** over in **search** of what he needs and **returns home** to **find it.**"

GEORGE MOORE

"One's destination is never a place,
but a **new way of seeing things.**"

HENRY MILLER

"We do not believe in ourselves until someone reveals that **deep inside us something is valuable**, worth listening to, worthy of our trust, sacred to our touch. Once we **believe in ourselves** we can **risk** curiosity, wonder, spontaneous delight or **any experience.**"

E. E. CUMMINGS

"The only way to make sense out of change is to **plunge into it,** move with it, and **join the dance.**"

ALAN WATTS

"**Change and growth** take place when a person has **risked** himself and **dares** to become involved with **experimenting with his own life.**"

HERBERT OTTO

"Some men see things as they are and say **why**—I **dream** things that never were and say **why not.**"

GEORGE BERNARD SHAW

"Human life is a **journey** whose end is not in sight. **Searching, longing and questioning** is in our DNA. Who we are and what we will become is determined by the questions that animate us, and by those we refuse to ask. **Your questions are your quest.** As you ask, so shall you be."

SAM KEEN

"Think impossible and dreams get discarded, projects get abandoned, and hope for wellness is torpedoed. But let someone yell the words **'It's possible,'** and **resources** we hadn't been aware of come **rushing in** to assist us in our quest."

GREG ANDERSON

"...live to the point of tears."

ALBERT CAMUS

"**Believe nothing** just because a so-called wise person said it. Believe nothing just because a belief is generally held. Believe nothing just because it is said in ancient books. Believe nothing just because it is said to be of divine origin. Believe nothing just because someone else believes it. **Believe only what you yourself test and judge to be true.**"

BUDDHA

"Life is no passing memory of what has been
Nor the remaining pages of a great book
Waiting to be read

It is the opening of eyes long closed
It is the vision of far off things
Seen for the silence they hold
It is the heart after years of secret conversing
Speaking out loud in the clear air."

DAVID WHYTE

"Twenty years from now you will be more disappointed by the things that you didn't do than by the ones you did do. So **throw off** the bowlines. **Sail away** from the safe harbor. Catch the trade winds in your sails. **Explore. Dream. Discover.**"

MARK TWAIN

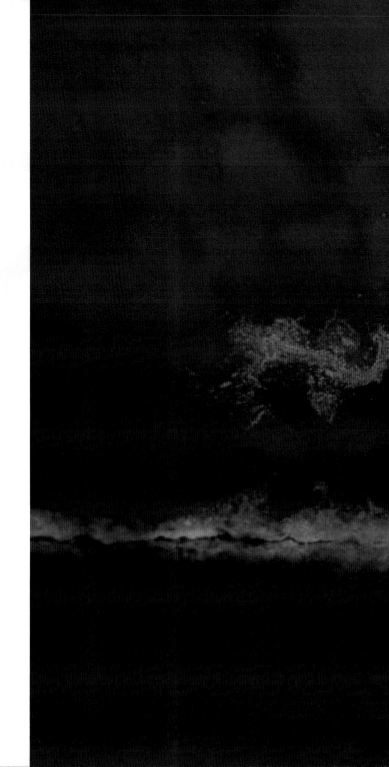

"This **world** is but a **canvas** to our imagination."

HENRY DAVID THOREAU

"The real **voyage of discovery** consists not in seeking new landscapes but in having **new eyes.**"

MARCEL PROUST

"To See a **World** in a **Grain** of Sand
And a Heaven in a Wild Flower,
Hold **Infinity** in the palm of your hand
And **Eternity** in an hour."

WILLIAM BLAKE

"We are each **gifted** in a unique and important way. It is our **privilege** and our **adventure** to discover our own **special light**."

MARY DUNBAR

"It is only with the **heart** that one **sees** rightly. What is essential is **invisible to the eye**."

ANTOINE DE SAINTE-EXUPERY

"Sometimes everything has to be **inscribed** across the **heavens** so you can find the **one line** already written **inside you**."

DAVID WHYTE

"Simplicity is the ultimate form of sophistication."

LEONARDO DA VINCI

"The visible
and the invisible

working together
in common cause,

to produce
the **miraculous.**"

DAVID WHYTE

"Have **patience** with everything that remains unsolved in your **heart**. Do not now look for the answers... **live in the question.**"

RAINER MARIA RILKE

"We don't receive **wisdom**; we must **discover** it for ourselves after a **journey** that no one can take for us or spare us."

MARCEL PROUST

"The only way to **discover** the limits of the **possible** is to go **beyond** them into the **impossible**."

ARTHUR C. CLARKE

"Do not go where the path may **lead,**
go instead where there is no
path and **leave a trail.**"

RALPH WALDO EMERSON

"There is no end.
There is no beginning.
There is only the **infinite passion** of life."

FEDERICO FELLINI

"Remember that **happiness** is a way of **travel**, not a destination."

ROY GOODMAN

"In matters of style, **swim** with the current; in matters of principle, **stand** like a rock."

THOMAS JEFFERSON

"Be **still** with yourself until the object of your attention **affirms your presence.**"

MINOR WHITE

"You have **power** over your **mind**—
not outside events. **Realize** this,
and you will find **strength**."

MARCUS AURELIUS

"Life is either a **daring adventure** or nothing.
Security is mostly a superstition.
It does not exist in nature."

HELEN KELLER

"When I looked at things for what they are
I was fool enough to **persist** in my folly
and found that each photograph
was a **mirror of my Self.**"

MINOR WHITE

"Peace.
It does not mean to be in a place with
no noise, trouble or hard work.
It means to be in the midst of those things
and still be **calm in your heart.**"

ANONYMOUS

"We see things not as they are, but as we are."

H. M. TOMLINSON

"Knowing yourself is the beginning of all wisdom."

ARISTOTLE

"May the **sun** bring you new **energy** by day, may the **moon** softly **restore** you by night, may the **rain wash** away all your worries, may the **breeze blow** new **strength** into your **being**.

May you walk gently through the **world** and know its **beauty** all the days of your life."

APACHE BLESSING

"**Gratitude unlocks** the fullness of **life...**
Gratitude makes sense of our past,
brings **peace** for today and
creates a **vision** for tomorrow."

MELODY BEATTIE

"The time will come when, with **elation** you will **greet yourself arriving** at your own door, in your own **mirror** and each will **smile** at the other's welcome, and say, sit here. Eat. You will **love** again the stranger who was your self. Sit. **Feast on your life**."

DEREK WALCOTT

"Some people come into our lives and quickly go. Some people **move our souls** to **dance.** They **awaken** us to understanding, with the passing whisper of their **wisdom.** Some people make the sky more beautiful to gaze upon. They stay in our lives for awhile, leave **footprints on our hearts,** and we are never quite the same."

ANONYMOUS

"In the **infinity** of life where I am, all is **perfect, whole, and complete.** I no longer choose to believe in old limitations and lack. I now choose to begin to **see myself** as the Universe sees me—perfect, whole, and complete. I now choose to **live my life** from this understanding. I am in the **right place** at the **right time**, doing the right thing. **All is well** in my world."

LOUISE HAY

"To improve the **golden moment** of opportunity, and catch the good that is **within our reach**, is the great **art of life.**"

SAMUEL JOHNSON

Photographer's Note

The photographs exhibited in *Coastal Inspirations* were made over twelve years, several after repeat visits to the same location at various times of the day and year to improve composition and lighting. Each image has its own storyline embedded in memory that accompanies it; a personal response to what is before me at the moment when the shutter is pushed. The joy of photography is exploring an area and discovering a subject that calls out. My image making intent is much more than a literal reproduction of the scene or object before me. The challenge is to convey the emotions felt at the time and have others respond.

All photographs were made with slow speed slide film and drum scanned without any enhancement, alteration, or modification. The rectangular sized images were shot with Nikon F3 and N90S 35 mm cameras and lens and the square images with a Hasselblad 203fe medium format camera and Zeiss lens.

Acknowledgments

This book would not be possible without the memories of our family growing up by the ocean. We would like to thank our immediate family, Patricia Herlihy and Jeff O'Neil, who have been instrumental in sharing our passion for the coast, a place were we call home.

During the development of this book, the images, quotes, pairings, and flow have changed multiple times. The evolution of the book came not only from our efforts but from the suggestions, reactions, and comments of dozens of friends and family members. To each, we are grateful for your feedback, causing us to pause and question the fit between image and quote. At each point along the way, we were driven by our desire to improve the quality of the book and viewer experience by broadening and intensifying the possible meanings left to resonate with the viewer's imagination and curiosity.

We are especially appreciative of the time and attention demonstrated by Jan Pogue publisher of Vineyard Stories and Jill Dible graphic designer. From the beginning, Jan and Jill understood our vision and transformed our photographs and words into a book of beauty and inspiration.

Thank you to all who have contributed to making our first book possible!